ON THE HUNT WITH
CROCODILES

SANDRA MARKLE

Lerner Publications ◆ Minneapolis

THE ANIMAL WORLD IS FULL OF PREDATORS.

Predators are the hunters that find, catch, and eat other animals—their prey—to survive. Every environment has its chain of hunters. The smaller, slower, less able predators become part of the prey for the bigger, faster, more cunning hunters. But everywhere, just a few kinds of predators are at the top of the food chain. These are the top predators. In the coastal ocean waters, rivers, and swamps of tropical parts of Africa, Asia, the Americas, and Australia, those top predators include crocodiles. Scientists have identified eighteen species, or kinds, of crocodiles and believe there may be more. The largest of these different crocodile species is the saltwater crocodile. A close runner-up is the Nile crocodile.

SALTWATER CROCODILE

NILE CROCODILE

NILE CROCODILE

Why are saltwater crocodiles and Nile crocodiles top predators? For one thing, they are big enough to hunt and kill their habitat's large prey, such as wildebeest. An adult male saltwater croc may be up to 23 feet (6.5 m) long and weigh as much as 2,200 pounds (998 kg). The largest adult male Nile croc may be up to 20 feet (6 m) long and weigh as much as 1,700 pounds (771 kg).

Female saltwater crocodiles and female Nile crocodiles are usually about half as long as and weigh much less than the males. Scientists aren't sure why male crocodiles grow to be so much bigger than females. One possibility is that males fight other males to win control over large territories for hunting prey animals. Or, like this Nile crocodile male and female couple, it could be to gain mating rights by fighting off other males. But even though they are smaller, female saltwater crocodiles and female Nile crocodiles are still big enough to hunt and overpower large prey.

MALE NILE CROCODILE

FEMALE NILE CROCODILE

WOW!
Nile crocodiles sometimes hunt together by lining up shoulder to shoulder to block a small creek or river section. Then they catch and eat any fish that swim into this trap.

NILE CROCODILE

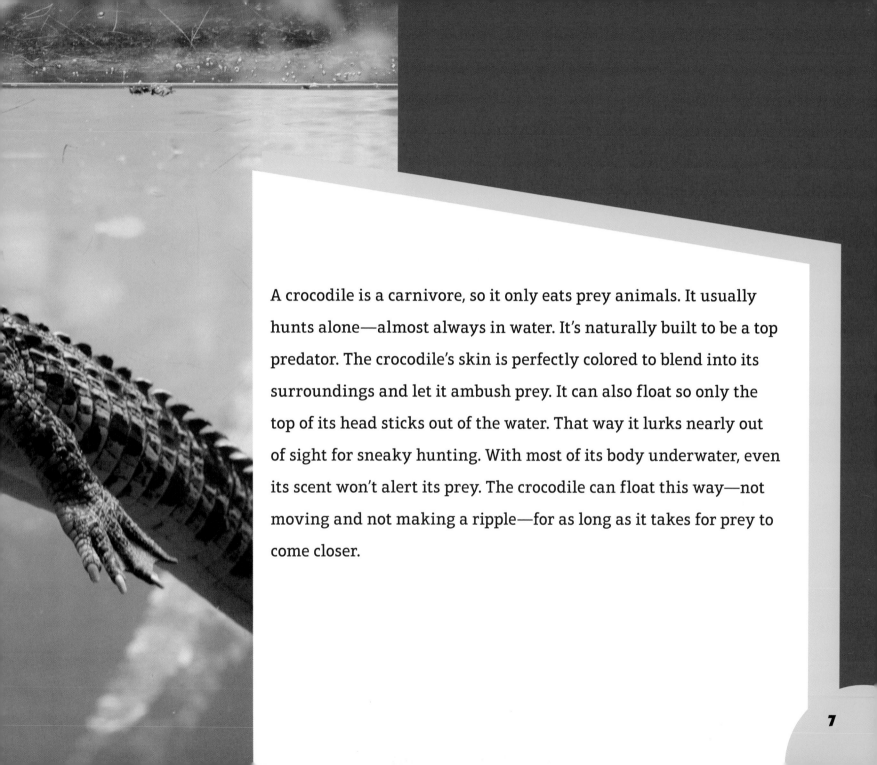

A crocodile is a carnivore, so it only eats prey animals. It usually hunts alone—almost always in water. It's naturally built to be a top predator. The crocodile's skin is perfectly colored to blend into its surroundings and let it ambush prey. It can also float so only the top of its head sticks out of the water. That way it lurks nearly out of sight for sneaky hunting. With most of its body underwater, even its scent won't alert its prey. The crocodile can float this way—not moving and not making a ripple—for as long as it takes for prey to come closer.

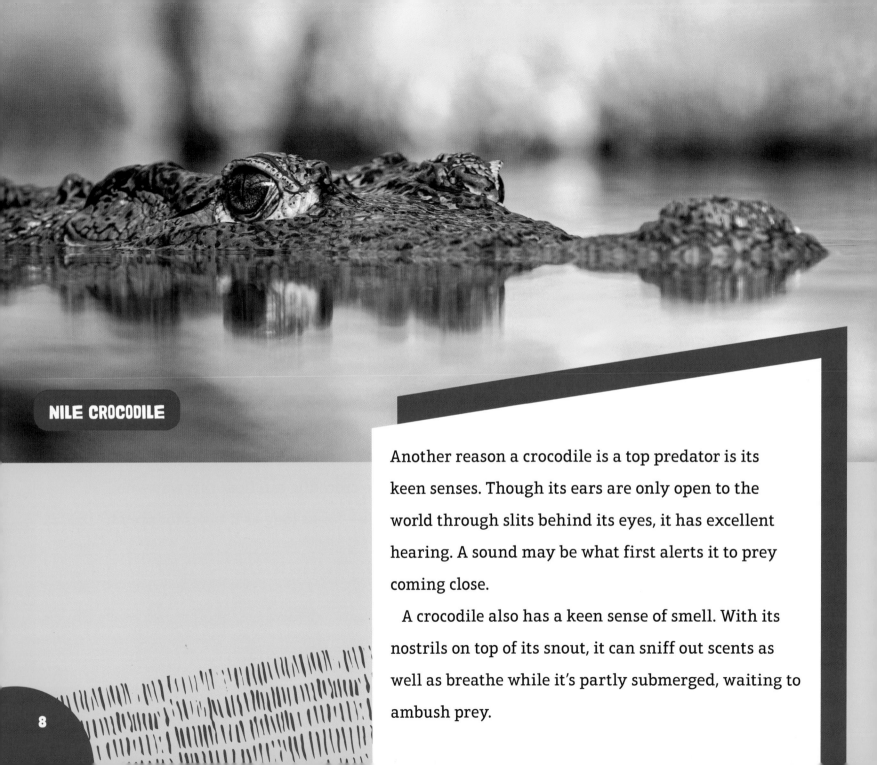

NILE CROCODILE

Another reason a crocodile is a top predator is its keen senses. Though its ears are only open to the world through slits behind its eyes, it has excellent hearing. A sound may be what first alerts it to prey coming close.

A crocodile also has a keen sense of smell. With its nostrils on top of its snout, it can sniff out scents as well as breathe while it's partly submerged, waiting to ambush prey.

But the sense a crocodile counts on most when hunting is its sight—even underwater. When the croc sinks below the surface, a third eyelid, called a nictitating membrane, slides over each eye. Like goggles on a human swimmer, this membrane protects its eyes from sand, dirt, and anything else in the water. But this special eyelid isn't completely see-through, so it limits the hunter's vision a little. Still, it protects the croc's eyes while it's sneaking close underwater to ambush prey.

NILE CROCODILE

Once the crocodile dives, a chemical in its body slows its heartbeat and shifts blood from its lungs to the rest of its body. This way the hunter can hold its breath and wait submerged for more than an hour for its chance to attack. But this time, it doesn't need to wait very long. Some of the zebras wade into the water close to where it's hiding.

Pulling its legs tight against its body, the torpedo-shaped croc slices through the water propelled by powerful sweeps of its long tail. Even before it surfaces, the croc opens its big jaws wide. It can do that because a fleshy flap of skin at the back of its mouth presses against a flap on the back of its big tongue. This creates a watertight valve, letting the croc grab its prey without swallowing water.

It's dinnertime!

WOW!
A crocodile can swim as fast as 20 miles (32 km) per hour for short bursts—much faster than even record-setting human swimmers.

NILE CROCODILE

11

NILE CROCODILE

Each of the crocodile's sixty-four to sixty-eight teeth averages 5 inches (13 cm) long. They are a strong cone shape with a sharp tip. All its teeth are perfect for biting and gripping. But it can't chew or grind up food.

To eat large prey, the crocodile holds it in its jaws, lifts the animal out of the water, and violently slings it to one side. The weight of the prey's body tears away what the croc isn't gripping. Then the hunter lifts its nose and tosses the torn-off chunk into its mouth down its throat. Ready for more, the croc swims to what's left of its prey and repeats the chomp, swing, and gulp process.

Such a rough way of catching and eating its food may cause the crocodile to lose teeth. But this top predator will always have a big, toothy bite. Any tooth that's lost is replaced by a new tooth slowly moving up from inside its jaw to fill the space. This happens regularly, so crocodiles always have their jaws armed with different numbers of teeth. Their teeth are also at different stages of moving into place, so many appear to be different sizes.

NILE CROCODILE

When it's done eating, a crocodile usually rests. It often crawls out of the water. Soaking up heat on a sunny bank helps its body have the energy it needs to digest its food. After a big meal, it may not hunt again for several days. But if it only caught and ate a snack, such as a fish, it will soon be hunting again— even if it's dark by then.

WOW!
When a crocodile gets too warm resting in the sunshine, it opens its big mouth to help it cool off.

14

NILE CROCODILE

Another reason a crocodile is a top predator is its skill at nighttime hunting, when being sneaky is easiest. It can hunt in such dim light because a crocodile's pupils, the openings that let light enter its eyes, can open extra wide. This lets as much light as possible reach the retina. That's the layer packed with light-sensing cells at the back of each eye. A mirrorlike layer behind the retina reflects light back through the retina again—back onto the light-sensing cells. This bounced light helps the croc's night sight, and it makes its eyes seem to glow in bright light.

15

SALTWATER CROCODILE

Whether its meal is big or only snack-sized, such as a turtle, the crocodile doesn't chew up its food, so its stomach has a lot of work to do. To process what it eats, the crocodile's stomach is a large sac with two different sections. It has a muscular part to mash up the food and a part that produces digestive juices to break down the mashed food. A crocodile's digestive juices are so powerful they even break down turtle shells, bones, horns, and hooves. The only undigestible animal parts are scraps such as feather shafts, some hair, and some bony scales, such as those on a garfish.

WOW!
A crocodile sometimes swallows small stones to help its stomach mash up its food.

MALE NILE CROCODILE

FEMALE NILE CROCODILE

18

After a big meal, a crocodile can go days or even a few months without eating. But if it gets a chance to catch prey, it eats—even if it has to fight other crocodiles for a share. Crocodiles need to eat to be active and to stay healthy. But they also need to eat to grow big enough to become mature and reproduce.

For crocodiles, reproducing is more about size than age. For example, female Nile crocodiles usually don't reproduce until they're about 7.5 feet (2.2 m) long, the size they reach when they are about twelve years old. Male Nile crocodiles usually need to be at least 10 feet (3 m) long, and they generally don't reach that length until they are about seventeen years old.

All mature crocodiles mate during their habitat's rainy season. Each mature male patrols his territory and drives away rival males. But he lets any female that enters his territory stay. If she swims close enough to bump against him, he pushes back. This is the beginning of their courtship. After mating, the female leaves. She has a big job to do!

A female saltwater crocodile crawls ashore and scrapes together mud, plants, and sticks to create a mound a little over 5.5 feet (1.6 m) wide and about 1.5 feet (0.4 m) tall. Digging down into the center of the mound, she creates a cavity where she deposits as many as one hundred eggs. Next, she scrapes some of the nest material over the eggs to bury them. But that's not the end of what the female will do for her babies.

WOW!
Saltwater crocodiles are very vocal, including barks, growls, chirps, and hisses.

SALTWATER CROCODILE

While the baby crocodiles develop inside their eggs, this female saltwater crocodile guards the nest from egg-eating predators. She even goes without eating to stay nearby and keep watch. How quickly the baby crocs develop depends on the weather—the warmer the weather the faster they grow.

After the first few weeks, the nest temperature also determines if the baby crocodile will become male or female. In parts of the nest that heat up and stay between 86°F and 90°F (30°C and 32°C), the babies become males. Where the eggs stay a little cooler—around 82°F to 86°F (28°C to 30°C)—the babies become females.

After developing for nearly three months, the baby saltwater crocodiles hatch. And they are noisy about it! Each baby yelps as it breaks out of its egg. Together, the hatchlings make enough noise that their mother hears them. She claws and bites away the dirt that has hardened to seal the nest cavity, freeing the hatchlings.

WOW!
Each crocodile hatchling is about 11 inches (28 cm) long and weighs around 2.5 ounces (72 g)—about three times bigger than the average baby chicken.

SALTWATER CROCODILES

A female Nile crocodile digs a hole to deposit her eggs. She uses her hind legs and snout to dig a hole in sandy soil. After depositing her eggs, the female Nile crocodile pushes dirt into the hole, covering the eggs. Then she guards her nest. Once the babies hatch, they make noise and their mother digs away the soil, releasing the hatchlings.

But the mother Nile crocodile's job doesn't end there! She scoops her new family into her big mouth—a few hatchlings at a time—and carries them to nearby water. Though her jaws are strong enough to crush bone, she won't even scratch a hatchling's skin.

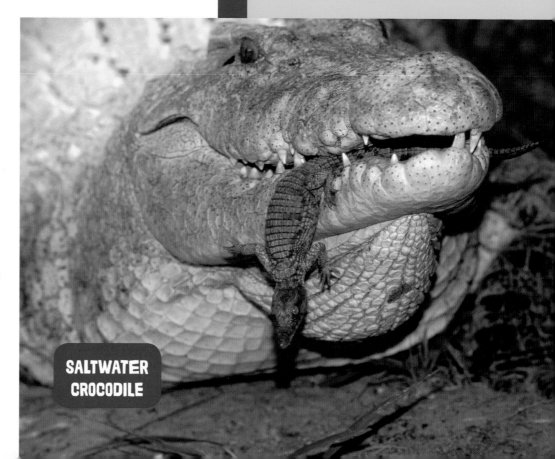

SALTWATER CROCODILE

The water where their mother releases them becomes the hatchlings' nursery. There, the young crocs have safety in numbers, being one of many clustered together. That's especially important when their mother is away hunting to feed herself and isn't guarding them. But she never goes far. So if a predator such as a wading bird comes close, the youngsters' distress barks bring their mother charging to the rescue.

The young crocodiles also quickly learn to catch their own food. They hide in the water by submerging all but their heads. Then, lunging, they snap their jaws to catch whatever comes close, including a dragonfly skimming over the water.

NILE CROCODILE

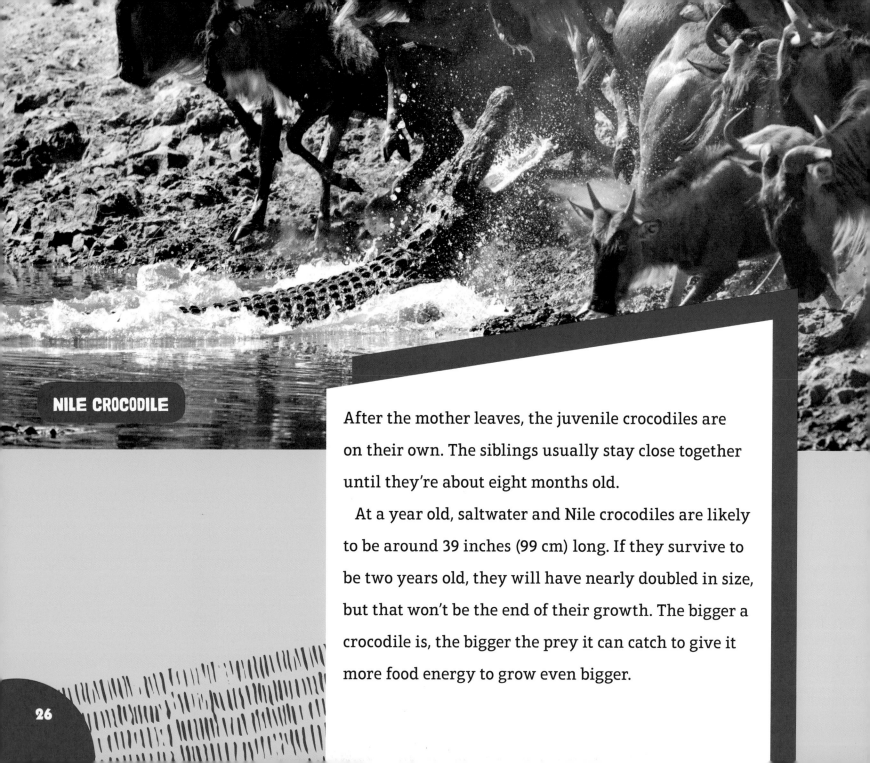

NILE CROCODILE

After the mother leaves, the juvenile crocodiles are on their own. The siblings usually stay close together until they're about eight months old.

At a year old, saltwater and Nile crocodiles are likely to be around 39 inches (99 cm) long. If they survive to be two years old, they will have nearly doubled in size, but that won't be the end of their growth. The bigger a crocodile is, the bigger the prey it can catch to give it more food energy to grow even bigger.

Eventually, each young adult crocodile claims a territory. There the crocodile will keep on hunting and growing even bigger as it becomes a top predator in its habitat.

NILE CROCODILE

A NOTE FROM SANDRA MARKLE

Even top predators face challenges, and global changes in Earth's climate are challenging saltwater crocodiles and Nile crocodiles in one big way. The areas where these animals live are getting warmer. Remember, the temperature of the environment heats up the crocodile's nest and incubates the eggs inside. So warmer nest temperatures could cause more of the babies than usual to become males. And since only females can produce eggs, a warming environment could, over time, cause crocodile populations to decline.

The warming environment is also challenging the survival of juvenile crocodiles. That's because they need to spend a lot of time submerged to avoid being caught by predators. But researchers have observed that young crocodiles stay submerged for much shorter periods in unusually warm water. So a warming climate puts them at a much higher risk of becoming prey before they grow into being top predators.

Photo by: Skip Jeffery Photography

SNAP FACTS

SALTWATER CROCODILES

ADULT SIZE
Males may be up to 23 feet (6.5 m) long and weigh as much as 2,200 pounds (998 kg). Females are usually much smaller.

DIET
They will eat anything they can overpower.

LIFE SPAN
In the wild, they live as long as seventy years.

YOUNG
Babies develop inside eggs in a nest for about eighty days before emerging as hatchlings.

RANGE
They roam saltwater and brackish (slightly salty) water areas of coastal eastern India, southeastern Asia, and northern Australia.

FUN FACT
When a saltwater crocodile attacks prey, its protruding eyes move down into their sockets to protect them. Then they pop up again.

NILE CROCODILES

ADULT SIZE
The largest adult male Nile crocs may be as much as 20 feet (6 m) long and weigh as much as 1,700 pounds (771 kg). Females are usually much smaller.

DIET
They mainly eat fish but will eat anything they can overpower.

LIFE SPAN
In the wild, they live as long as eighty years.

YOUNG
Babies develop inside eggs in a nest for about eighty to ninety days before emerging as hatchlings.

RANGE
They mainly live in freshwater rivers, lakes, marshes, and lagoons of Africa and western Madagascar.

FUN FACT
On land, a young adult Nile crocodile can push up to raise its body off the ground and gallop for a short distance.

GLOSSARY

CARNIVORE: an animal that only eats other animals

EGG: a structure within which a baby crocodile develops

FOOD CHAIN: a series of living things where each is dependent on another as a source of food

HABITAT: an animal's natural home range

HATCHLING: a baby crocodile

NEST: a hole a female Nile crocodile digs to deposit her eggs before covering them with dirt; a mound a saltwater crocodile builds to deposit her eggs before covering them with nest material

PREDATOR: an animal that hunts and eats other animals

PREY: an animal that a predator catches to eat

TERRITORY: the water and surrounding land where a crocodile usually hunts and defends from other crocodiles

INDEX

Image credits: Ariadne Van Zandbergen/Alamy Stock Photo, p. 3 (top); DEA/C.DANI/I.JESKE/agency/Getty Images, p. 3 (bottom); Andre Gilden/ Alamy Stock Photo, p. 4; USO/iStock/Getty Images, p. 5; Tibor Bognar/Alamy Stock Photo, pp. 6–7; Arterra Picture Library/Alamy Stock Photo, p. 8; imageBROKER/Alamy Stock Photo, p. 9; BIOSPHOTO/Alamy Stock Photo, pp. 10–11; CORREIA Patrice/Alamy Stock Photo, p. 12; Rob Walls/Alamy Stock Photo, p. 13; gerard lacz/Alamy Stock Photo, p. 14; PhotoStock-Israel/Alamy Stock Photo, p. 15; Joao Inacio/Moment/Getty Images, pp. 16–17; CMH Images/Alamy Stock Photo, p. 18; Stephen Lloyd Malaysia/Alamy Stock Photo, p. 20; Jorg Spannhoff/Alamy Stock Photo, p. 23; Avalon.red/Alamy Stock Photo, p. 24; Mark Deeble and Victoria Stone/Getty Images, p. 25; Andre Gilden/Alamy Stock Photo, p. 26; Christian Hutter/Alamy Stock Photo, p. 27.

Cover: Bernard Radvaner/Corbis/Getty Images.

THE AUTHOR WOULD LIKE TO THANK DR. KENT A. VLIET, UNIVERSITY OF FLORIDA, GAINESVILLE, FLORIDA, FOR SHARING HIS ENTHUSIASM AND EXPERTISE. A SPECIAL THANK-YOU TO SKIP JEFFERY FOR HIS LOVING SUPPORT DURING THE CREATIVE PROCESS.

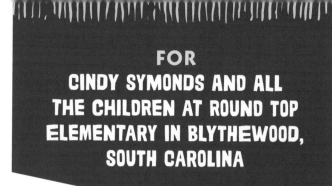

FOR
CINDY SYMONDS AND ALL THE CHILDREN AT ROUND TOP ELEMENTARY IN BLYTHEWOOD, SOUTH CAROLINA

Lerner Publications Company
An imprint of Lerner Publishing Group, Inc.
241 First Avenue North
Minneapolis, MN 55401 USA

For reading levels and more information, look up this title at www.lernerbooks.com.

Main body text set in Aptifer Slab LT Pro medium.
Typeface provided by Linotype AG.

Editor: Brianna Kaiser

Library of Congress Cataloging-in-Publication Data

Names: Markle, Sandra, author.
Title: On the hunt with crocodiles / Sandra Markle.
Description: Minneapolis : Lerner Publications, [2023] | Series: Ultimate predators | Includes index. | Audience: Ages 8–12 | Audience: Grades 4–6 | Summary: "Crocodiles are near the top of the food chain. They have keen senses that make them excellent hunters. Readers will learn all about them, from how they find prey to how they train their young"— Provided by publisher.
Identifiers: LCCN 2021045419 (print) | LCCN 2021045420 (ebook) | ISBN 9781728456232 (library binding) | ISBN 9781728464374 (paperback) | ISBN 9781728462400 (ebook)
Subjects: LCSH: Crocodiles—Juvenile literature. | Predatory animals—Juvenile literature.
Classification: LCC QL666.C925 M3746 2023 (print) | LCC QL666.C925 (ebook) | DDC 597.98/2—dc23/eng/20211013

LC record available at https://lccn.loc.gov/2021045419
LC ebook record available at https://lccn.loc.gov/2021045420

Manufactured in the United States of America
1-50693-50112-1/24/2022